D1526840

Complete guide to

I walk of Santiago

de Compostela

From the passion for pilgrimage combined with the experience gained from countless walks and treks around the world, comes the essential guide to spiritual and physical preparation that will help you overcome your fears and better face the journey that will change your life.

Walking-Trekking-experience-2023

Complete guide to the Camino de Santiago de Compostela - 2 books in 1 + the French way

Copyright © 2023

2023 edition

Author: Fabio Pedaci

The book

LAO TSE WROTE FROM A JOURNEY OF A THOUSAND KILOMETERS ALWAYS BEGINS WITH ONE STEP. THE FIRST STEP. THIS IS THE ONLY ONE THAT COUNTS BECAUSE WITHOUT THE FIRST, AS WITH BREATHING, THERE WILL BE NO OTHERS, BECAUSE IT MARKS A GAP. FROM EVERYDAY LIFE, FROM LOVED ONES, FROM COMFORTS, FROM ONE'S HOME, FROM WORK.

<u>Your first step in embarking on this wonderful journey is:</u>

Thinking about it_ in this phase, the mind begins to fantasize about all the emotions and experiences that will follow during the journey. You begin to give it your own interpretation and it increases that determination that will lead you to live a completely unique and personal experience

Designing it_ to leave prepared, giving space only to the emotions of an itinerant experience, limiting unpleasant hitches along the way to a minimum. Good preparation increases awareness of what you are doing and makes everything easier and more enjoyable. Like when you face high school exams… if you are prepared, you get better results.

Living it_ realizing your thoughts, letting yourself be carried away by emotions to make a load of experiences that will significantly change your life.

<u>The journey begins with the thought but does not end when it returns, well it will remain indelible within you!</u>

How long have you felt this irrepressible desire to set off on the Camino de Santiago but are you tormented by a thousand questions and doubts? Well, it's time to take the first step!

In this updated edition you will find in detail all the answers to the questions that most first-time pilgrims ask themselves. There will also be useful advice for those who have already done the journey but want to improve their approach to it.

Some of the topics covered:

- **historical notes on the origins:** so that you can understand the importance of the journey

- **description of the 9 main routes:** in order to help you choose the one that best suits you
- **mental approach:** in order to ensure the achievement of the established goal without the risk of motivational collapse, to enjoy only the beauty of the journey.

- **Physical preparation:** thanks to simple exercises to perform before departure, you will prepare your body to face the journey, minimizing the classic injuries that pilgrims normally encounter

- **What to pack:** practical advice for leaving a light, technical equipment, clothing, beauty case, and everything you need, leaving at home what you probably need because you won't!

- **Choosing the right shoe:** advice on choosing and its importance. The wrong one could compromise the journey

- **Economic budget:** to get an idea of the costs to be incurred, with some tips on how to save

- **How to organize the stages:** advice on how to deal with them day by day based on their characteristics.

- **The French Way:** detailed guide of every single stage and of the places present on this way, up to the Cathedral of Santiago. Including detailed map

- **The Albergues:** Advice on the choice of structures to stay with the description of the various types present on the way

- **Useful info:** useful applications that can be downloaded to your smartphone. Path Maps. Pilgrim credentials. And much more

INDEX

Chapter 1

How it all began

In recent centuries, the Camino de Santiago has become a point of reference as well as a place of worship for Christianity because through different itineraries, mainly in Spanish and Portuguese territory, the final destination is the Spanish city of

Santiago de Compostela, located in the region of Galicia; here, inside the cathedral of Santiago, the remains of Saint James, **one of the apostles of Jesus, are kept**.

The history of the Camino de Santiago has old roots wrapped up in history but inevitably also in legend and perhaps this is also one of the reasons why we are still fascinated today.

The Path of the Stars

As the name itself says, the Camino de Santiago originates from the **veneration for St. James** the Greater, the first, among the twelve apostles of Jesus, to have been martyred for his adherence to the Christian faith; in fact, he was beheaded under the orders of the then king of Judea, Herod Agrippa. Subsequently, the other apostles succeeded in stealing the body of the Saint and crossed the whole Mediterranean until reaching the coasts of modern Galicia for the following eight centuries all traces of the remains of the Saint were lost until, around 813 AD, a hermit named Pelayo, following **a particularly bright star**, reached the foot of Mount Libradòn where he discovered a tumulus. He made the bishop of the area Teodomiro aware of the find and the identity of the

Apostle was attributed to the remains. One of the theories on the origin of the name of the city of Santiago de Compostela is based on this legend: it is in fact from this field indicated by the stars that the name *Compostela would have originated*. Subsequently, the King of Asturias Alfonso II the Chaste was informed of the incident, established that St. James would become the **patron saint of the kingdom,** and ordered the construction of a church in the place of discovery. The legend, according to which an apostle is buried in Spain, suddenly became a reality, thus instilling new strength in the Christian faithful throughout Europe.

In fact, a series of victories by the various Spanish kingdoms followed and were attributed to the protection of the Apostle. Thus the legends of Santiago *Matamoros,* or " ***the Moor-Slayer*** " spread.

For fear that pirates would take possession of the relics at the end of the sixteenth century, they were hidden and for almost three centuries they were considered lost.

In 1879 they were founded and officially recognized by Pope Leo XIII.

In the middle of the story of the Camino de Santiago

Calixtinus a guide, a book from 1139 contains a detailed explanation of the culture and the various stages of the French Way.

From 1179 there was an increase in pilgrims due to the fact that Pope Alexander III granted an indulgence to those who had arrived in Santiago until it reached great popularity in the last two centuries of the Low Middle Ages with the discovery of the remains of St. James

The Way in our age

At the end of the Middle Ages the Way held a second-rate position despite the fact that pilgrimages did not stop. One of the many reasons why the path was abandoned came from the diffusion of the Enlightenment and its concepts; we recall the criticism of Erasmus of Rotterdam who argued that pilgrims excessively exhibited faith.

Two other events followed to make the Way even more difficult; first, the Protestant Reformation which involved the closure of the borders of the Catholic kingdoms, including Spain, to prevent access to the Protestant heresy, and follow, in 1589, the moving of the relics of the Saint to a secret place to prevent the English, led by Francis Drake, invaded Galicia and robbed them.

We remember the Italian priest, from Bologna to be precise, Domenico Laffi as one of the most important characters of the pilgrimage for the vast amount of information he provided on the journey he traveled in 1666, in 1670, and in 1673. The pilgrims of the time relied on the guidance of his book "Viaggio in Ponente a San Giacomo di Galizia and Finisterre, Bologna, 1673".

The contemporary Way of St. James

In 1879, with the rediscovery of the relics of St. James, the pilgrimage to Santiago de Compostela slowly resumed and then reached its climax in 1982 with the visit of Pope John Paul II.

From here, adequate signage began to be introduced along the way, along with the creation of reception facilities and services along the entire Way.

In 1993, the Camino de Santiago has then declared a World Heritage Site by Unesco; the number of pilgrims made up of people of all nationalities and all languages began to steadily rise every year to make this pilgrimage, reaching the enormous number of 347,578 people as declared in the 2019 Camino de Santiago statistics.

Jacobean Holy Year

In the history of the Camino de Santiago, the Holy Years that have followed one another over the centuries has always held very great importance, both from a religious, cultural, and political point of view. But what is a holy year?

Whenever July 25 falls on a Sunday, the so-called Jacobean or Jubilee year is celebrated in the city of Santiago de Compostela. The frequency with which this event takes place is every six, five, six, eleven years, and so on: for example, in 2021 and then in 2027, 2032, 2038, 2049. The inauguration takes place with the opening of the Holy Door (photo above) of the cathedral of Santiago on 31 December of the previous year, during which the archbishop of the city, using a silver hammer, struck the wall facing the door three times from the outside.

From now on, this Door will remain open throughout the year of Compostela and will be the entrance that pilgrims will use to enter the cathedral. As you can see, the immense cathedral of Santiago has many doors, but the Holy One is very special. This is the " Puerta del Perdón ", or the "Door of Forgiveness", which overlooks Plaza Quintana and which you will normally always find closed, except precisely in a holy year.

For those who are devout and for those who in any case attribute a religious significance to the Way, whoever crosses the holy threshold will gain complete forgiveness of their sins. Also for this reason, in the history of the Camino de Santiago, the celebration of holy years has always played an extremely important role, given the fact that the number of pilgrims on the way has always undergone a dizzying increase when this particular event occurs.

The pilgrim: from the Middle Ages to the present day

The pilgrim was mainly associated with a religious person who carried out a journey of faith and an act of devotion towards a holy place by traveling this road praying and performing rites in honor of God.

Many pilgrims walked the Camino de Santiago following the commission of sin as a penance or imposed by the judges who considered it a suitable mode of expiation for a punishment committed

Other pilgrims walked the path to request grace or healing for a sick relative.

The pilgrim already from those times dressed in a particular, very specific way:

- The dress shouldn't have been too long so as not to get caught in the branches;
- He carried a bag containing only the indispensable, he had to rely on divine providence.
- He wore a hat to protect himself from the sun and rain.
He carried a wooden staff which served as support and support in the most difficult moments.
He had a canteen made from a gourd, worn at waist level or attached to a cane;
- He possessed a weapon to defend himself against thieves or animals.
- He had a small leather bag for money and the contents had to be visible, testifying to the pilgrim's trust in providence.

An important aspect to consider is that the journey on foot started from one's home and had to end exactly there, thus lasting months or years and entailing a considerable sacrifice also from an economic point of view.

Many pilgrims sold part of their belongings before leaving; they were also aware of having to face many pitfalls; brigands, dangerous animals, and bad weather. For this reason, before leaving, they prepared a will.

Chapter 2

The first step is to think about it

How many times have you promised yourself to do something, even just a weekend away or a trip of a few weeks, whether it is from stories learned in some documentary, from the stories of someone who has lived exciting experiences or even just the fruit of your unconscious, and you have thought could be interesting and rewarding for you, that it could help you to increase your experience and maybe if you want to pass it on to your loved ones and friends, well, already the fact that you have thought about it and that you think about how to implement what you have in mind is your starting point, and since you are reading this manual it means that you are starting to plan and implement what you have in mind to make sure that it does not remain just a dream, that YOUR Way to Santiago de Compostela becomes reality, or better still I would say that you are preparing to live your daydream, because it is no coincidence that it is said that the journey is magical, it is no coincidence that it is said that along the way you meet p fantastic people and places and that once finished, once you reach your destination you cry for joy, and when you return home and to everyday life you realize the change and the many positive effects this wonderful journey has had on you

Every reason is valid

From what we have learned, the Way to reach Santiago de Compostela was born purely for religious reasons, however today it is estimated that pilgrims who undertake this journey driven by religion are increasingly in the company of those who have chosen to do it for other reasons far from They; in fact, you meet people driven by the most disparate but equally valid motivations; in fact, along the way you will find those who set off on this adventure for reasons: sentimental following a separation from your partner with the need to leave everything behind and then start again, there are those who are looking for their other half and in many cases also succeed to find it, those who want to find themselves and others the need to get lost and let go for a certain period, those who simply do it out of a spirit of adventure and want to replace the classic organized holiday at least once in their life with a traveling adventure and the desire to wake up every day in a different place, those who want to put themselves to the test to reach and overcome their limits and fears by fueling their self-esteem, those who want to spend some time alone to find moments of deep reflection or on the contrary to be among people finding yourself in wonderful companies where you can share your experiences of life with people from all over the world who are culturally distant from their own, some do it for sport, some to immerse themselves in nature, etc. etc. etc., in short, we could go on and on with the list to try to identify a shared reason but the truth is that there is no one that is more valid than another, and whatever yours is, it is certainly right to start.

The spiritual benefits of the Way

If we think that the best philosophers of ancient Greece such as Aristotle, Socrates, and many others, taught their disciples their theories by walking under the arcades, there was probably a reason, in fact, walking leads to a condition favorable to learning and thought, the quiet of the walk favors the elaboration of concepts better and creates the conditions for looking at oneself in the third person as there is a clear detachment from the everyday routine, whether it is from work or family life. Let's consider that at the time the theory was spreading that "The act of walking stimulates the human being in an active form of meditation that solicits the participation of all the senses, one walks for no reason, for the simple pleasure of enjoying the time passes, to discover unknown places and faces, or simply to respond to the call of the path". Walking we learn to reinvent time and space and teach us to have happy humility before the world.

Obviously embarking on such a desired experience, so meditating, studying, and planning down to the smallest detail, leads to having reasonable expectations. We expect that at the end of the trip, there will be something that is worth having spent our time and money on having undertaken this adventure.

Surely the mere fact of going out for a more or less long period from one's comfort zone of everyday life to which we are accustomed entails having a spirit of adaptation in the face of the circumstances one faces, one finds oneself adapting to times and thoughts different from ours, dictated by places, paths, people and the sharing of their culture and experience, a bit as if we were looking out of a window from which we see a world made up of many colors, some of them probably not we hadn't even seen them until today, and we could also realize that in the end, not only the colors that we were used to seeing are beautiful just because we are addicted to habits, it is enough to change the perspective even just a little and we realize that in the end life is full of colors, shapes, cultures, thoughts and ways of living to discover and interpret, basically you just need to change your perspective to realize that to open up to the living world or experiences different from those we are used to can bring enormous physical and mental benefits.

Along the way, we will realize the weight of the many superfluous thoughts that we carry with us, how much time we waste and intoxicate our mind by sacrificing ourselves to have such a complex and difficult lifestyle to achieve and maintain when in the end the most beautiful things are almost always the simplest. Some thoughts that emerge when the departure is approaching and we prepare the backpack can be:

Will I be able to stay away all this time from a specific object that is part of my daily life?

How do I start without having solved that problem I've been thinking about for a long time?

And the work to carry on?

My family and friends?

What about my physical limits? Etc. etc..

Well, making the journey helps to change perspectives and put the mind in order, to recognize and overcome one's limits, and heal wounds. We realize that after all that object from which we never detached ourselves is of no use to us that much, that that problem seemed so difficult to overcome because they always tried to do it with the same method, you will return full of joy and with a spirit of optimism such as being able to pass it on to your loved ones who will be happy to learn about your experiences and get infected by your happiness. Along the way, we really realize what is important to us and what we can easily do without it, that the physical and mental limits in most cases were those imposed by ourselves

During the Camino we will realize that ultimately the goal is not Santiago, but the Camino itself

Chapter 3

All roads lead to Santiago de Compostela

The routes to reach Santiago are really many, but in reality, the most organized and busy one is the French one which alone attracts over half of those who arrive in the renowned city every year, pilgrims who inexorably continue to increase over the years so much that in the months between May and July, the last 100km of the stretch are congested, it can be said that Santiago somehow moves a flood of pilgrims. But let's see some statistics.

How many Pilgrims have completed the journey and collected the Compostela (the diploma that certifies the pilgrimage), in the years between 2009 and 2019:

- 2009: 145,877 pilgrims.
- 2010: 272,135 pilgrims.
- 2011: 183,366 pilgrims.
- 2012: 192,488 pilgrims.
- 2013: 215,880 pilgrims.
- 2014: 237,983 pilgrims.
- 2015: 262,516 pilgrims.
- 2016: 277.85 pilgrims.
- 2017: 301,036 pilgrims.
- 2018: 327,378 pilgrims.
- 2019: 312.72 pilgrims.

To these must be added those who are not interested in collecting the Compostela for various reasons.

What are the most popular paths in 2019, and who has traveled them

CAMMINO	NUMERO PELLEGRINI	%
Cammino Francese	189937	54,65
Portoghese	72357	20,82
Portoghese Costa	22292	6,41
Del Nord	19019	5,47
Inglese	15780	4,54
Primitivo	15715	4,53
Via de la Plata	9201	2,65
Muxia-Finisterre	1548	0,45
Cammino d'inverno	1035	0,3
Altri cammini	694	0,2

The Pilgrims arrived in Santiago result

- 26.75% are under 30 years old
- 54.52% were between 30 and 60 years old
- 18.73% from pilgrims over 60 years old

With an almost equal distribution between the sexes?

With regard to nationalities, we find pilgrims arriving from all over the world, led by the hosts with around 42% of presences, followed by Italians with 8%, Germans with 7%, the United States with 6%, and others including Asian and South American countries

Which path to choose

Here the choice is very subjective, certainly, all the routes listed have to give emotions but some may be more suitable and tailor-made for you.

At the landscape level they are all valid, in some cases such as the Portuguese coast and the northern one there is the possibility of seeing the ocean and the sea, while the others develop in the hinterland and offer varied landscapes ranging from the countryside to the mountains passing through some great Cities. The physically more demanding ones are certainly the primitive, the English, from La Plata and from the north, these are also less frequented and organized in terms of accommodation, they cross fewer cities and consequently offer fewer services, inevitably entailing leaving slightly more organized and respecting the established stages more rigorously than the other routes where you can afford to have greater flexibility and decide according to your needs whether to lengthen or shorten the established stages.

While the French and Portuguese Routes are the most assorted in accommodation and services as they pass through some important cities, as well as being, as seen in the statistics, the most popular ones.

At this point, on the basis of the descriptions and statistics listed, some considerations should be made such as:

- How much do I want to be in company and share the road with other pilgrims? If the desire to share prevails, undoubtedly French followed by Portuguese are the most suitable, the fact remains that if you want or need to be alone for a while, there is also the possibility here, even if it can happen to find crowded accommodation.

- How many spirits of adaptation and energy do I have inside me? If we are aware that we lack these requirements, it would be

advisable to avoid choosing the routes that
are more demanding and less popular

Having made these reflections, you will see that
the answer comes by itself, and whatever path you
choose is certainly the right one, because it was
chosen by you!

NB. All the routes are well signposted, even the less
frequented ones, consequently, the possibility of
getting lost involuntarily is low!

How many days does it take

Live on the Camino without haste. Enjoy every place, every person, every moment. Live it as the journey that can change your life. He will do it!

It is clear that, apart from some categories ranging from pensioners to seasonal workers, from students to the unemployed, the number of days available can be a problem for an active worker. On average, the days it takes to get to Santiago by walking the various routes in a reasonable way, without haste but fully enjoying all that they have to offer, are different for each route, dictated by the distances and difficulties that characterize them.

The time estimates for the main routes considering average stages of about **25 km per day** are

I walk	Departure city	Total km	Stages/days
French	St Jean Pied de Port	757.5km	30
Portuguese	Lisbon	613.4km	24
Portuguese coast	Lisbon	643.9 Km	27
Of the North	Irùn	816.6km	34
English	Ferrol	115.4km	6
Primitive	Oviedo	313.6km	14
Via della Plata	Seville	978.2km	36
Muxia Finisterre	Finisterra	110Km	4
I walk in winter	Ponferrada	262.7km	10

The table shows the routes in full, starting from the cities of origin.

Many pilgrims change the starting point according to the days they have available, in order to shorten the kilometers to go and still arrive in Santiago. The fashion that has been gaining ground in recent years is to do the last 100km of the French course starting from the city of Sarria, but we need to reflect on this " If it is true that even the last 100km are worthwhile and give emotions, that somehow you manage to savor the spirit of the pilgrim, and it is also true that (especially if we are talking about the French Way), not starting from the city of origin you miss the most beautiful part, the most spectacular sunrises, the breathtaking landscapes that change during the journey and the different welcome of the people who live in the various places that you cross. In a nutshell, doing the last km is comparable to seeing only the end of a great film, it can have an exciting epilogue but you haven't seen the plot and you have to get it told".

What to do if the days available don't allow you to walk the Camino you have chosen in its entirety? - Simple! do it in stages, if you only have 10 days available and you want to make a journey that requires 30 you will finish it in three years, every year you will pick it up where you left off the year before, without a hurry, always remember that the journey is there that has been waiting for you for centuries, and will always be like this.

With whom to walk the Camino

Organized trip? In recent years, with the constant increase in pilgrims, the journey has become a business attraction also for some tour operators and organized groups, but having such an experience in a group, with obligatorily established stages and times, means that they lose the taste for adventure and lose what is the spirit of the pilgrim. My advice is to avoid taking the walk by treating it as a classic trip!

With friends or family? It can be done but the risks of something going wrong should not be underestimated.

I have met many people who left as friends and returned as friends at the end of the journey! In essence, the greatest threats to the affection of a friendship or a relationship derive from a few factors:

- Firstly, from the walking step. Having the same as your travel companion is not obvious and forcing your own pace more or less fast, adapting it to those next to us involves sacrifices and increases the possibility of physiological injuries. Consequently, if you choose to walk the route with someone, you need to accept the fact that if the pace is different, especially in the more demanding stages, there may be a certain detachment along the way and then meet again at the end of the stage.

- <u>Do not underestimate the physical resistance</u>. Everyone has their own! Once a roadmap with well-defined stages has been jointly established, it is not certain that it will be able to be respected. In fact, it can happen that due to minor injuries, simple physical tiredness, or any other reason, there is a risk of changing the established stages, creating disagreements and bad moods among travel companions.

<u>The different interests that can attract us during the journey are related to</u> places, moments, and monuments to visit. Enjoying everything the path offers is the prerogative, living it in an exclusive way catapults you fully into the spirit of the pilgrim. Let's start from the concept that what is beautiful is not beautiful but what you like, i.e. a place, a monument, a landscape or anything else that can attract your attention may not be the same for someone else, beauty in many cases

is subjective and in some, it triggers such admiration that they want to dedicate a certain amount of time to it. For example, if along the way you feel like stopping for a few hours to observe a breathtaking landscape or smell the scents that some woods have to offer, or even if you simply feel like contemplating the sea, are you sure that your travel companion wouldn't turn up your nose? What if, crossing a town or a city, you realize that it has more to offer than you thought, and it would almost be worth stopping one more day to visit it? You would break the shared roadmap!

Those listed are just a few factors that can play against undertaking a journey with friends and family, of course, there are also some positive notes in doing it with someone but it is essential that if you decide to leave with a friend there is awareness of the fact that there are no people who are 100% compatible with one's being, that being touchy can compromise the journey, it is essential to face the journey without any mental cage, agreeing to respect the will of one's travel companion without impositions.
In summary, the real risk we run is that of becoming each other's ballast.

Alone? It is the most preferred starting condition of pilgrims. During the journey, it often happens to meet those who by choice walk in complete solitude, but you also meet many close-knit groups, formed during the same journey by individuals who had set off alone.

Clearly, the choice to go alone has its great advantage, and unlike those who go with a company, you don't have to account for what you do to anyone but yourself. You are free to take all the time you want to go through your stages, stopping where you want and if you feel like changing them to your liking and according to your needs. Take all the time you think necessary to admire that spectacular sunrise, have breakfast in a hurry or very calmly if you decide what is worth seeing, how much time to dedicate to a place and where to stay for the night, with the privilege of being able to change idea, even without valid reasons whenever you want.

And if you want you will never be alone, the people you will meet on the way are each special in their own way, in many cases ready to socialize and with a particular spirit of inclusion. As already mentioned, many small groups are created along the way, join them if you feel like it, and do it harmoniously and with extreme dynamism, but remember that once you have established an inevitable emotional bond with the various components, it will happen, trust me! letting yourself be conditioned in some choices and actions along the way is normal and understandable, but feeling obliged to respect the choices of others is not. So my advice is, join them if you want, walk with someone only if you find someone who doesn't force you to force your pace, feel part of the group, but always remember that if you are left alone to feel free from impositions.

If your intention is to go it alone, don't be held back by the fear that if something happens to you, any kind of problem, you will find yourself facing it alone. Because the people you will meet on the way are united by a very special spirit of solidarity, it is extremely difficult for a pilgrim to leave others in difficulty, and you may be surprised to see the determination of those you meet in giving physical and moral support to all those who they need it.

With my 4-legged friend? As feasible as it is, in reality, pilgrims with their dogs following them do not meet many. However, those who intend to leave in the company of it must take into account some aspects: first of all, the accommodations that accept animals are few; some paths could be dangerous for him; remember that he doesn't wear shoes, and in the warmer months he could suffer a lot in those few hot sections of asphalt that you come across, or he could even cut himself on the rocky sections. But the real question is.. are you sure your friend really wants to do this?

How much does it cost to walk

In reality, how much to spend on the journey is up to you, in the sense that the costs vary a lot according to your needs and the spirit of adaptation that you manage to have. Of course, there is a minimum of expense to be faced related to transport, food, lodging, and obviously everything concerning the equipment put in the backpack.

But let's start with some examples:

- Making a prediction regarding the cost of how to get to Spain is difficult, it really depends on your city of origin and the means of transport you want to use. If your option is to take one of the many low-cost flights, once you arrive in Spain we can realize that, unlike Italy, take for example Bologna where the cost of the shuttle to and from the airport costs around € 9, Madrid or Santiago costs €1.20, a 300 km journey by bus costs only €17, so once you arrive in Spain, reaching the starting point of your journey by public transport is really cheap.

- The accommodation? In general, to rest the pilgrim uses structures exclusively dedicated to the category called Albergue, there are various types and the costs vary from 8 € to 14 €, in addition to the Albergue with a fixed rate, there are also many so-called "donativi", which provide a liberal donation. This does not mean that if you have special needs, you will also find the classic accommodation facilities dedicated to tourism with prices adapted to the categories clearly higher than those of the Albergue. (while reading this guide you will find details about the Albergue)

- The food? Here too there is a lot of space, how hungry and thirsty are you? Normally the physical effort required to tackle the journey increases the body's demand for liquids and food in a subjective way. Then there is the possibility of choosing to refresh oneself in accommodation facilities or in supermarkets to consider, obviously there is a natural difference in spending between the two. But let's take a few examples:
A good sweet or savory breakfast made at the bar can cost between € 4 and € 5; at the market around €2.
Lunch at the bar/restaurant if you limit yourself to a sandwich or soup with a drink,

stay around € 6-7; at the market a sandwich costs € 2 on average.

Dinner at a restaurant or in an Albergue, many establishments have a menu dedicated to pilgrims which usually costs around €12 and includes 2-3 courses, wine, water, and dessert included in the price. In some Albergues, there is also the possibility of using the kitchen, and with a cost of 3-4 € at the market you can make yourself a big salad and a plate of pasta, or of course, take what you like best.

- The prices of some products consumed at the bar: a small draft beer served with a tapas (snacks) €1.20, cost about the same for refreshing canned drinks, natural orange juice €1.5-2.5, a portion of empanada stuffed) €4-5, a portion of tortilla (omelet with potatoes) €2-3, coffee €1.2. Water at the bar costs €1 for half a liter, but almost always the water flows into the public and potable network and tastes good.

In wanting to make an average expenditure of only the costs of food and lodging, considering a typical combination: sleeping in Albergue spending an average of 10 € per night, breakfast and dinner in the accommodation facilities, lunch at the market, a few refreshed drinks and a snack, we are around the figure of **€ 32-37 per day**. You can clearly spend much more if you are looking for more services, but also less if you adapt and have fewer needs.

NB: The prices shown refer to the French route, they are to be understood as an average and subject to some variations by the regions that are crossed

Chapter 4

Physical and mental preparation for the Camino

We assume that you are not leaving to do a competitive competition, an Everest climb, or any other extreme sport you can think of, none of that. If we really want to give it a place on the road, we could define it as something that goes beyond a simple walk, mixed with a marathon without competition due to the physical resistance required, with a pinch of mountain trekking. Therefore, no type of exaggerated training is required, but some simple exercises aimed at protecting the areas most stressed during walking and preventing some injuries certainly help.

Prevent and treat the most recurring walking injuries

The injuries that can be found in the activity of any prolonged walk are usually minor; however, some can be so annoying that they compromise or at the very least slow you down.

The most common injuries encountered while walking are:

Foot blisters are certainly in first place among the most common evils in pilgrims. The triggering cause of these is the continuous rubbing between the skin and the shoe, and between the skin of the toes themselves.

To prevent them there is no preparation to be made months before leaving, but some precautions are to be implemented during the same journey and consist in treating the skin by applying creams based on zinc oxide and magnesium silicate, or simply white Vaseline (widely used among pilgrims).

It involves distributing the cream over the entire sole of the foot and between the toes, applying it in the evening before going to bed, and in the morning before putting on socks; in this way, the skin acquires greater softness and the friction with the socks decreases. The choice of socks is of fundamental importance, these can really play a decisive role on the path as if you wear the right ones you could significantly limit the onset of blisters. All you need to do is go looking for anti-blister socks and you will find all kinds, but in my opinion, the characteristics that these must have are that they adhere well to the foot, limit rubbing with the skin, have a good thickness, be free from annoying seams, have a small percentage of merino wool or other components useful for limiting foot perspiration, and if you opt for socks with toes, all the better, also eliminate rubbing between them and what this entails.

But all possible precautions may not be enough, and if you were predisposed some blisters could come anyway. So how to cure them? The classic and conventional method is to use a special plaster competed with a gel inside designed to absorb the liquid from the bladder to dry it, the contraindication is that it increases the volume of the affected area resulting in discomfort, and in some cases it can come off by tearing part of the affected skin, thus making the blister itself worse. Another less conventional but extremely decisive method is to use a needle to pass a cotton thread from side to side of the bladder and leave it inside with its head and tail a few cm long from the entry and exit holes, placing above it a plaster. In doing so, the thread will act as a drainage by drying the liquid inside the bladder, significantly shortening the healing time. **Attention**, to avoid the onset of infections, it is advisable to disinfect all the components used, including the affected skin, with a special disinfectant, such as Betadine. (although this last remedy with a needle and thread is very successfully used on the road, the detail given in this guide is not advice in applying it and the author declines all responsibility).

On the lower limbs. Among these tendinitis and heels, articular resentments affect the ankles and knees, calf muscles, and quadriceps with the risk of overload contractures.

Clearly, each of us has a degree of physical preparation and a different structure from the other. In the event that you do not exercise regularly, in order to limit the risk of injury, it would be advisable to perform some simple preparation exercises useful for better tackling the Camino.

Start training 4-5 months before, do it consistently, and stop a week before leaving.

One of the best exercises to tackle walking is simply walking at a fast pace, this doesn't mean you have to walk before walking, but simply just do 12/13 km outings 2-3 times a week. For those who are not really used to walking, even just 10 km can be tiring, just remember that your body has to get used to it, don't give up, and have faith in yourself, you will gradually get used to it and you will move your limits further, and going 10 km will seem a stroll.

To strengthen the quadriceps it is sufficient to do a few squats and push-ups, and increase the intensity gradually but without stressing the muscles too much, you will not have to do a body-building competition.

Ankles and calves, after blisters, are in second place of the ailments that afflict pilgrims on the way.

The main problems of ankle injuries tend to be small sprains and fatigue of the surrounding muscles, and derive from the repetitive movement of the feet carried out on uneven and accidental terrain. While the calves usually bring pain and in some cases tears and contractures due to prolonged exercise overload.

Recommended exercises to help strengthen calves and ankles can be the lifts on tiptoes, the use of the proprioceptive table, the elastic, and everything that stimulates the muscles concerned

On the other hand, regarding the ligaments of the knees, those who already have history usually suffer, if you are aware that you have some little problems, you can evaluate the idea of walking with a knee brace from the beginning and even before it gets inflamed. However, there are some

simple exercises that can help strengthen the adjacent muscles and give greater support to the knees, and they are mainly those performed in gyms with the leg press, openings with elastic bands, and even the bike does its part.

As regards heels and tendonitis, these are already starting to be more complicated to manage than by taking drugs. Usually, those who suffer from these problems are those who have got the wrong shoe and find themselves with a too-stiff sole, but we will go into more detail on the "shoe" issue in the chapter dedicated to the choice of clothing.

IMPORTANT: Stretching before and after the stage is essential, the time you dedicate to it will certainly be rewarded by a better state of muscle health.

NB: in some cases, anticipating makes the difference, if you even suspect you have vulnerable points, protect yourself with everything you can, if you think that your ankles may be weak, then start already with anklets, or knee pads if you have weak knees, etc..
Don't wait for the clinical picture to get worse, if you feel pain from inflammatory states taking an

anti-inflammatory can be decisive, remember that you're living your own path, and it's an experience you don't always have!

In case of mineral salt deficiencies, especially in the warmer months when we expel them in large quantities through sweating, the additional intake of magnesium and potassium may be important to counteract exhaustion and muscle cramps.

Mind and Spirit feed the Physique

Many times already after the first steps we feel tired, we realize we have small pains or something annoying, and well if we had to listen to all these small signs we will never do anything, we will stop immediately at the first signs losing all the opportunities that they are waiting for. Yet, we almost never stop at the first symptoms, we listen to them as it should be, it is correct to listen to our body, the difference then lies in giving the right interpretation to the signals it gives us, understanding what it needs, if it throws a tantrum or no, and it happens that sometimes he becomes lazy and has little desire to do. Of course, you are the mind and as such you govern the body, but He is the one who takes you for a walk and without it you physically go nowhere, so if there are disagreements what do you do? Well... there is a compromise if he wants to stop before your mind, find an agreement, go halfway further than the one who wants to do the physical and halfway less than what the mind wants to do, but only if he accepts the compromise, never force his will too much, but try to gradually move the existing limits, both of the body and of the mind. The mind is smarter than the physical, and logical and rational actions are expected from a smarter being.

While you will do the Camino and you will sometimes feel tired, exhausted, and no longer have the strength to go on, you may even think that you will not be able to reach your destination and you will start thinking "but who made me do it?!", remember that if it was you who decided to do it for a very specific and extremely valid reason, yours! You, therefore, have a motivation that will take you to Santiago, and don't worry if you end up feeling destroyed, the next day you will be amazed at how your body will meet you, how you will be able to recover the energy that seemed to have disappeared the day before. And step by step, day after day you will feel that self-confidence increase, and you will notice how your mind and body have empathized with each other, you will begin to acquire more and more awareness of who you are. able to do, because the journey gives you everything you need.

Whether you understand it from the beginning, during, or at the end, you will discover that the effort of the journey that seemed so hard to you was actually worth it, it is worth all the sacrifices spent, and the tears you will shed when you arrive in front of the Cathedral of Santiago will give you the confirmation!

Chapter 5

The backpack

If we can face a months-long journey with only what we carry in our backpack, then what is left out is superfluous.
 (cited by Francesco Grandis)

Without taking it too literally, we could think there is some truth in Grandis' words!

There are people who actually spend months away from home with only what they have in their backpack, maybe they will miss something they have left at home, but all in all, they manage to do without it.

They have become able to adapt to what they have, which is in any case the essentials, and having only the essentials is the best condition to face this journey lightly and with a free mind.

Once you get familiar with your backpack, you'll realize that you'll find it hard to stay away from it during the journey and it will become your best travel companion. So when you go to buy it, get a good and suitable one for you, you have to feel it is yours otherwise continue in the search.

Let's start from the assumption that not always spending a lot is synonymous with quality, but for a good backpack the average cost is between €70 and € 140, it depends a lot on the brand you are going to buy and the aesthetic finishes, as well as the materials used.

Technical characteristics of the backpack: the search categories for the backpack are obviously those for Trekking, hiking, and hiking, to fit everything you need inside comfortably, a 45l is enough. Check that the shoulder straps and the belt are well padded so that the weight will weigh as little as possible on the shoulders and the belt that wraps around your waist will be comfortable. Some backpacks also have a perforated mesh on the back in order to ventilate the area and avoid excessive sweating. More or fewer pockets to your liking, the lighter the better!

Furnish it externally with the pilgrim shell
And if you want, customize it with the patches you like best!

You can buy the shell**, the credential**, and other gadgets online at:

https://www.santiagodecompostela.me/collections/best-selling-it

Or alternatively in the shops you will meet along the way and in some Albergues!

What do I put in my backpack

Everything you need! removing what you probably need, because you won't need it!

The best pilgrims manage not to go beyond 6 kg in weight, the average is 8kg, the less skilled or more demanding ones, if we want, manage to weigh it beyond that. When preparing your backpack, remember that you have to carry it on your shoulder, that you are not going to war and if you need something in Spain you will still be able to find it, so avoid carrying objects on your shoulder that you will probably never use.

Considering that you will wash your clothes almost every day, whether it is for a week or a month, let's give a practical example of what a pilgrim's backpack should contain when leaving between April and September:

Clothing

"In addition to what you will wear on the day of departure"

- 2 shorts, preferably in technical fabric, of which at least 1 can be converted into long trousers to be used in cool or damp weather.

- N°2 T-shirt preferably in technical fabric

- 2 pairs of socks, preferably anti-blister, those with toes help prevent rubbing between the toes and limit the onset of blisters

- N°2 briefs preferably in technical fabric. If you are prone to chafing in the groin area, I highly recommend using those specially created to remedy this problem, they are simply longer than the classic boxers.

- A thermal shirt, especially useful on high-altitude routes.

- A sweatshirt or technical jacket, preferably with a hood and fleece lining.

- A light pajama.

- A hat or bandana to protect you from the sun.

- A swimsuit. It happens to find hotels and villages with swimming pools or rivers available for pilgrims.

- A pair of Sandals, preferably in Eva material due to the very low specific weight. To be used both in the shower and to replace shoes at the end of the stage.

- A dispenser bag can be useful where you can insert all the clothing in such a way as to have them in order and practical to take them from inside the backpack.
- A small bag for dirty clothing

In the beauty case

- What is needed and required for oral and personal hygiene, but in a travel format. An out-of-stock product is easily repurchased along the way.

- White vaseline or emollient and anti-friction cream, to be applied at least twice a day on the feet.

- Nail clipper. Remember to always keep your toenails very short to prevent them from causing bruising and pain to the toes due to the repeated crushing action with the shoe, especially when going downhill.

- Laundry soap. Among pilgrims, it is customary to use Marseille soap both for washing clothes and for washing oneself. Alternatively, for personal hygiene, there are 200g shower shampoo bottles.

- In the warmer months, sunscreen may be useful.
- For women, if you just can't go without makeup, bring only the essentials.

Other

- Light sleeping bag as an alternative to sheets, in this case, a small plaid can be useful. Consider that the albergues provide disposable type sleepers for the mattress and pillow, and only in some cases also blankets.

- Trekking poles; which really make the difference on paths with unevenness and rough ones, as in addition to giving greater stability and balance, they also offer the possibility of distributing forces by discharging inertia also on the arms. It is good to bear in mind that if you intend to reach the departure point using the aircraft, this equipment is not allowed to be taken on board in the cabin, consequently, you will be obliged to store it in the hold. Considering that this equipment is also easily found on the route at prices between 20-30 €, therefore evaluate whether it is convenient to bring them from home or buy them on the spot and then perhaps leave them as a gift to some other pilgrim.

- Earplugs. Resting well is important, and the cot neighbor is not always silent.

- Microfibre bathrobe or beach towel, plus a small towel.

- Led light, indispensable for departures in the dark.

- Some clothespins and safety pins are to be used in case you need to finish drying the clothes on the backpack during the journey.

- Needle and Thread

- Some medicine not to be unprepared. As easy as it is to find a pharmacy in Spain, it can happen that when you need it it is closed or there are none nearby. So bringing just a little Ibuprofen and Tachipirina could be an advantage (consult your doctor first). Plus some Band-Aids and some disinfectant. In case of sprains or muscle fatigue, in Spain, there is a very valid and widespread cream among pilgrims called Radio salil, which constantly inebriates the dormitories of the Albergues with its strong perfume.

- A pouch or small backpack (the resealable nylon ones), in order to carry your personal documents and the most important things with you once you arrive at your destination and deposit the backpack.

- A bottle or a bag of water of at least 0.8l. Fountains and bars are not lacking on the route, but it is advisable to always travel with a sufficient load of water, so fill up whenever you have the opportunity.

- The credential of the Camino de Santiago. It would be an accordion-shaped booklet that has the function of recording, using the various stamps that will be made by the Albergues, Cathedrals, and available structures present along the way, the stages and kilometers traveled by the pilgrim himself, so that he can go and request the Compostela one once arrived in Santiago. There are many different credential stamps and some may not have room for all stamps, in which case you may need a second credential. Once you arrive in Santiago, present them both to collect your Compostela.

- You can purchase the **credential online at:**

https://www.santiagodecompostela.me/collectio
ns/best-selling-it

Confraternity of San Jacopo di Compostella .it

Alternatively, in the Albergues and Cathedrals on
the Way

Now you have a backpack, you can Go!

Choosing the right shoes

The choice of shoes is certainly one of the most
important components, in fact, an unsuitable shoe

can make a difference during the journey, and contribute to the onset of injuries.

The mistake that many make is to think that the path is equivalent to a trekking excursion, and consequently many buy the shoe dedicated to this type of activity. In reality, there is very little trekking along the way, if we consider the French route, it can be deduced that approximately 7-8% of the entire journey approaches this activity.

A good compromise can be found by turning your attention to a trail running shoe, which in addition to having some characteristics similar to trekking shoes such as: ensuring good adherence to the ground and giving good stability to the foot, also has a very thicker, which allows you to better cushion the step and the roughness of the ground, resulting in a more performing stride and limiting the onset of heels, tendonitis and pain in the sole of the foot.

One of the most frequent doubts among pilgrims is whether to take shoes in waterproof fabric such as gorotex or breathable; high to better protect the ankles or low?

It depends a lot on the period in which the trip is faced, if we leave in hot months with little rain, personally I would avoid making my feet suffer in a shoe that is not very breathable and mostly high, moreover, it would be heavier for obvious reasons. Of course, even in summer it can rain, but I can bring shoe covers for the rain with me, and anklets to protect my ankles.

It is important to break in your shoes before setting off on the journey so that your feet get used to them, you can use them in the preparation walks you will take, but be careful not to wear them out too much...

Information notes:

- The choice of garments in the technical fabric allows them to dry much faster, a significant aspect considering that you will have to wash them almost every day.

- Almost all Albergues have washing machines and dryers available, which can be used at an average cost of € 4-5. To limit waste, pilgrims often share these services. Almost all the structures have special manual washhouses and drying racks for clothes.

- In most stages, there is a backpack transport service. It consists of taking it from the facility where you are staying and taking it to the next one you will go to. The cost of the service is 4-5 € which you will have to put inside an envelope, which you will ask the Ospitalero (the one who manages the Albergue) together with your data and your next destination. It is essential to notify those who offer the service using the contact you will find on the same envelope. I recommend using this service only if you really feel the need, you will miss it even if you hate its weight.

Chapter 6

The departure

<u>The mind and spirit are already on their way, you will soon join them!</u>

After a week you are now ready, and you can't wait to get on that plane or any other means that will take you to your starting point, you have stopped training to rest your muscles, but you can't stop your mind, think of all the useful details to tackle the journey, you've already tested the backpack, you'll have filled and emptied it several times, weighing it and trying to figure out if there's anything to add or take away.

Just do one last thing before calming all your thoughts and putting yourself in standby mode until the day of departure; considering that the day dedicated to travel is not usually walking, therefore evaluate based on the number of available facilities and your arrival time at the starting point, if it is useful to book a bed for that night.

The departure is imminent and you may be wondering: what will the first day be like? who will you meet on your way?
Your first day will likely be spent realizing that your dream is about to come true, and it will be more about the journey to get to where you started.

The first day

It's a bit like the first day of school, you look around and start observing and socializing with your classmates. More or less the same thing happens for the pilgrim, already at the airport you look around to see if there are people wearing details attributable to the category, and it often happens that you meet them. But only once you have arrived at your destination and taken your seat in the Albergue will you realize that you have entered a travel category that is unusual to the one you are used to.

However, when the time comes to spend the first night, you will probably have already met other pilgrims, dined, and exchanged words with some of them. You will have discussed the first stage to tackle the next day and you will have an idea of where to stay.

However, the time has come to rest and prepare to face your first stage.

How to organize stages

Organize them as you see fit, feel free to give it your own interpretation but be aware of some factors and consequences.

Among the aspects to take into account to ensure that the stages are pleasant and do not become particularly tiring, as well as of course making them proportionate to one's physical abilities, there is the correct evaluation of the choice of departure time. Let's start from the assumption that in any case, the structures dedicated to pilgrims require a free bed by 8:00, and in most cases, the pilgrims have already traveled quite a bit by that time.
To make a correct assessment of the departure time and ensure that you arrive at the end of the stage around the time you wish, it is necessary to take into account the:

- How many kilometers are you going to travel?

- How demanding it is based on the differences in height that characterize it.

- What is your average walking pace, including the breaks you are used to taking?

- If during the stage there are attractions that are worth dedicating time to

- During the hottest periods of the year, it's good not to underestimate the time of exposure to the heat of the sun. Walking in the hottest hours is equivalent to multiplying by far the energies and efforts necessary to face the path; therefore, leaving early in the morning can prove to be a decisive choice in order for the stage to be pleasant. Not to be confused with setting off at night, in fact, a stage traveled mainly in the dark, it excludes the vision of landscapes, nature, and everything that the same stage has to offer. In this case, it is good to find a fair compromise

- Accommodation is also important. Facts As already reiterated in some periods of the year, there are a certain number of pilgrims and it can happen that at the end of the stage in which you intend to stop, there is no place to sleep or in any case not in the structure you want, consequently, you may be forced to lengthen or shorten the stage, or alternatively adapt to the accommodation you can find, (it may also happen that you spend the night on the floor of some Albergue because in that country there is no bed available anywhere else, and you don't have the energy to go on or you don't want to stay behind in the village that precedes it. In any case, even if full, the Albergues always find accommodation).

However, it must also be said that many structures accept reservations, so if you are quite sure of the stage you intend to travel to and where you want to sleep, you can easily try to book a bed the day before or at least the same morning.

The structures that do not accept reservations are usually those called " Municipal ", which open at times ranging from 12:00 onwards (slightly variable depending on the management), and apply the rule of "first come, first served". , consequently, if you arrive late it is easy not to find an available bed.

The Albergues

They will be your point of support throughout the journey, the place where you will rest and take care of yourself, each of them will have different characteristics, harmonies, spaces, and rules. However, they all have the same goal of hosting the pilgrims in giving them refuge and refreshment, in order to contribute to the recovery of sufficient energy to face the next stage until reaching the goal of Santiago.

The Albergue distributed along the way differ substantially in three categories:

Private: managed as the definition itself says they are managed by private individuals and consequently they establish the price of the bed in complete autonomy, however, the cost usually remains competitive and on average low, in fact, it is between 10 € and 14 € for a bed in a shared dormitory, and in some cases, they offer the possibility of sleeping in single, double or quadruple rooms at a price which is obviously higher and which is around € 20-25. These structures tend to have slightly smaller shared dormitories than the Albergue managed by the Church or by the Municipals, and it is possible to find some more comforts such as the swimming pool, bar, and restaurant service.

Municipal and/or parochial: unlike private structures, these are managed by volunteers called hospitaleros, ordinary people who tend to have also had experience in pilgrimages but who nevertheless do much more in life and have chosen to dedicate part of their free time to doing this type of experience completely free, and for a limited period of a couple of weeks a year.

Dedicated facilities can belong to the church or to public institutions such as municipalities.

In the case of the church it, therefore, has a parish management, consequently finding a Sister as Hospitaleros rather than a Friar or a Parish Priest is usual, as it is for the dedicated structure to be a former convent or in any case, places dedicated to religion.

While for the municipal ones, are structures born or reconverted for the purpose and managed by volunteers through the coordination and subsidies of some public associations and institutions.

In both types of establishments, it is more difficult to find single rooms or in any case with few beds, just as it is probable that they do not accept reservations for the bed and consequently use the rule of first come, first serve.

Another of the rules that characterize these is that of the closing time which is usually set between 22:00 and 23:00, so keep it in mind if you happen to be in a city where you intend to be late in the evening.

Regarding costs, some of these structures apply a fixed rate for sleeping that is around €8, while others manage to apply the Donativo formula, i.e. give what you think is appropriate for your pockets in consideration of what you have used. Unfortunately, due to the lack of common sense of some and due to the increasingly high management costs of the same structures, this formula is starting to be scarce with the consequent rise in average prices per bed. My invitation is therefore to always give conscientiously.

If the path you have chosen is poorly equipped with accommodation along the way, you can always ask to sleep at churches, and fire stations and consult the locals, you will always find a place to rest because hospitality is part of the local culture.

Regardless of whether it is private, municipal, or parish, you will still find a way to rest, wash, wash, and dry clothes, and common areas useful for aggregation or even being alone.

Notes:
Some book a bed for all the stages of the journey, if you have this intention consider that if it is true that by doing so you will take away your worries during the journey, it is also true that you are already leaving with impositions that could deprive you of the freedom to change your mind about times, friendships and places to visit along the way.

The journey can also be technological

The path is a school of thought! It has been practiced since maps were scribbles reserved only for those who had the skills to decipher them, up to the present day where above us we have hundreds of satellites ready to locate us and give us support through handy applications.
Whether you want to do it the old-fashioned way without the help of technology or by taking advantage of them, the journey still has its value.

If your option is to take advantage of these, and not because there is any risk of getting lost or not finding sleep, but simply to make your life easier, know that there are some applications that you can install on your smartphone or sites to consult which certainly make the difference, can in fact:
list the various facilities along the route showing you their direct contact details, locate you on the route you are taking in real time, tell you how many km you have done and how many are left to reach your destination, how demanding the next stages are the services available on the route, and much more.

Among the most used by pilgrims to be installed on Android and Apple systems completely free of charge, we can find:

- Ninja path

- Happy Camino

- Gronze. com

Chapter 7

The French Way

The French one is undoubtedly the prince of the paths, the most popular, organized, and probably the most suggestive of the paths.
Its starting point is the characteristic French village of Saint Jean Pied de Port, located at the foot of the Pyrenees and considered the capital of the ancient Basque historical region of lower Navarre.

During this Way of over 800 km, you will cross five wonderful Spanish regions which differ from each other in terms of climate and landscapes, as well as the emotions and moods you will experience during the journey.

1st Stage Saint Jean Pied de Port - Roncesvalles
Length: 25km Total height difference: 2205 mt

It is in fact one of the most demanding and evocative stages of the whole journey.
This first stage includes the crossing of the Pyrenees, and even if it is really tough, the landscape and nature that make it up will greatly reward you for the tiredness and sacrifices made to overcome it.
Furthermore, weather permitting, you will have the opportunity to walk on clouds... It will be nice to sneak into the middle of the free pastures and smell the scents and the mountain breeze.
Until you arrive in Roncesvalles (**Navarre region**), where you will realize that you have truly begun your journey, you will have crossed the border between France and Spain and tasted the mystical magic of the Pyrénées-Atlantiques.
Roncesvalles is chosen by many pilgrims as a starting point in order to avoid the " leg-breaking " section consisting of the steep 1500m climb of the

Pyrenees, a route which in any case if you do not have particular physical problems it would be a pity not to do it, also because…. The satisfaction of going through what Napoleon's entry into Spanish territory was in his day is no small thing.

In this village of few souls, there aren't many structures, but surely you will be able to find a place in the hostel for pilgrims of Roncesvalles. If you want, in the evening in the church there will be a mass with the blessing of the pilgrim.

2nd Stage _ Roncesvalles - Zubiri
Length: 21.4Km Total height difference: 1239mt

Leaving Roncesvalles, the first icon you will find will be the much-photographed signage indicating the distance of 790 km to Santiago. Continuing you will cross Espinal, a typical Pyrenean village founded by King Tobaldo in 1269. Before arriving in Zubiri you will cross a Gothic bridge where according to tradition if an animal is affected by rabies by circling the central pillar of the bridge 3 times, it heals.

This second stage is certainly less demanding than the first, but it must be taken into account that the body still has to get used to the weight of the backpack and the kilometers covered, consequently, it is probable that this, as well as the next 7/8 stages, could be perceived more demanding than they really are, be patient and your body will get used to this condition.

3rd Stage _ Zubiri - Pamplona
Length: 20.25Km Total height difference: 904 mt

A particularity of this stage is the fact that it crosses many bridges over the Arga River and green areas, but as you approach the city you will notice that the landscape clearly becomes more influenced by civilization.
Pamplona is the first real city you come across on the way, and it is also the capital of the Navarre region. This is one of the liveliest and busiest cities along the way, so if you have the desire and energy to enjoy its nightlife, don't forget to stay in structures with no time limits in the evening.
Being a large city full of services, you can check your backpack and, if necessary, get rid of the superfluous using the shipping service, buy or replace what you need.

4th Stage Pamplona - Puente la Reina
Length: 23.9Km Total height difference: 1040 mt

Leaving cities is always particular, you grind kilometers and you have the feeling of not going forward, it's the effect of urbanization. The main objective of this stage is certainly to reach the top of the Perdòn, *located* on a hill at a height of 735mt. *el camino del viento con el de las estrellas* (Where the path of the wind crosses with that of the stars), which recalls both the constant wind that blows on the hill and the legend of the discovery of the tomb of the apostle James (indicated by a star to the hermit Pelayo in 813).
While it's not a particularly long stage, its steep climbs and slippery descents will make it quite challenging.
Once in Puente la Reina, thanks to the essence of the journey fully preserved in this city, you will find a way to regenerate yourself to face the next stage.

5th Stage Puente de la Reina - Estella

Length: 21.99Km Total height difference: 963 mt

This stage is not particularly demanding, it crosses an ancient Roman road, bridges, and rivers that also feel ancient.

The landscapes previously composed of cereal fields are gradually replaced by olive trees and colorful vineyards, in addition to the poppies and wheat present in the medieval city of Estella.

6th Stage_ Estella - Los Arcos
Length: 21.4Km Total height difference: 857 mt

Stage characterized by landscapes made up of woods, olive trees, and some abandoned stretches. Apart from the climb to get to Villamayor, it is very similar to the previous stage in terms of commitment.

However, it should be noted that once you leave Estella, a few kilometers away in the village of Ayegui there is one of the most particular attractions of the journey, in fact, you will find a fountain that instead of water dispenses wine, and a sip of nectar it can only do good.

7th Stage_ Los Arcos - Logrono
Length: 27.7Km Total height difference: 1023 mt

We say goodbye to the Navarre region and enter the Rioja region, famous for its wines considered the best in Spain. In itself, the stage is more demanding than the previous one due to the steep slopes, but once we have tackled the Pyrenees, nothing can worry us anymore. The city of Logroño as well as Pamplona is one of the great ones on the French Way, it also offers leisure opportunities and available services, and do not forget to take at least one tour of the famous Tapas street of the city's:

8th Stage_ Logrono - Nàjera
Length: 28.27Km Total height difference: 761mt

Certainly a long but not very demanding stage due to the route made up of moderate slopes. The colorful landscapes characterized by vineyards, fruit trees, and streams will make the walk particularly pleasant.

Once in Nàjera, you will notice its particular morphology, surrounded by red rocks and a river that flows at its feet, which will make your stay special and suggestive.

9th Stage Nàjera - Santo Domingo de la Calzada
Length: 20.9Km Total height difference: 642mt

We leave Nàjera to head towards the town of Santo Domingo, where the legend of the rooster and the chicken is in force, which tells of the two animals that, ready to be tasted by the governor of the place, together with a young man who was unjustly hanged, resurrected and went away with your own legs.

From this derivation the famous phrase "***Santo Domingo de la Calzada, whence the hen después de asada sang!*** **" (Trans.** *"San Domenico della Calzada, where the hen sang after being roasted"*).

To this day it is still customary to keep the two animals in a cage inside the Cathedral and in the municipal albergue, but I warn you that in the Municipal in the morning they sing their hearts out quite early.

10th Stage_ Santo Domingo de la Calzada - Belorado
Length: 22.7Km Total height difference: 599mt

In this stage we leave the region of La Rioja to enter that of Castilla y Leòn. Among the things that will catch the eye, there will certainly be the rivalry between the two provinces that you will find expressed on the stone blocks along the way. Even the landscapes will begin to change and the colorful vineyards will gradually give way to huge fields of cereals. This stage as well as the previous one will not be particularly demanding due to the moderate altitude differences that characterize it.

11th Stage_ Belorado - San Juan de Ortega
Length: 23.9Km Total height difference: 740mt

This stage offers predominantly mountainous landscapes and is made up of solitary roads which, with their trees and the murmur of the leaves, will create the ideal conditions to abandon one's thoughts and immerse oneself in meditation. Not a very demanding stage and if you manage to meditate along the way you will arrive in San j. (village with less than 50 inhabitants) Without even realizing it

12th Stage_ San Juan de Ortega - Burgos
Length: 25.97Km Total height difference: 575 mt

We head towards another of the important cities along the way, it won't be one of the big ones but it has its historical importance. Indeed, in the 11th century, it was named the capital of the kingdom of Castile and offered its visitors the grandiose Cathedral of Santa Maria de Burgos, designated a World Heritage Site.
The route to get there is quite simple, and once you get to Orbaneja, there is the possibility of taking a detour that will let you enter the city along the Arlazòn river, so as to avoid crossing the industrial area.

13th Stage Burgos - Hornillos del Camino
Length: 20.8Km Total height difference: 430 mt

After Burgos you will begin to concentrate on the silence of your steps and to understand the importance of patience which will accompany you in the next stages… Welcome to the Spanish Mesetas.

Immense expanses of wheat fields in the middle of nowhere where arid landscapes prevail and the yellow color are the master, the paths characterized by slight ups and downs almost as if they wanted to cradle you, and no shelter from the sun and cold or rain.

The Mesetas must be interpreted in the right way to appreciate them, sometimes silence can be harmful and as such, it can be harmful or spiritual, you decide which of the two.

14th Stage Hornillos del Camino - Castrojeriz
Length: 19.4Km Total height difference: 480mt

Stage very similar to the previous one, as will be the next until you get to Leòn until then you will cross small villages beaten by the sun and the cold. If the journey is done in the summer, the advice is to leave early in the morning to avoid the hottest hours.

15th Stage_ Castrojeriz - Fromista
Length: 25.2Km Total height difference: 597 mt

We continue our long and patient journey through the monotonous but always evocative landscapes of the Mesetas until we reach Fromista. Alternatively, in the summer, stopping 5 km before the destination at Boadilla del Camino to take advantage of the swimming pool made available by the En el Camino Hostel could be regenerated.

It is customary for pilgrims, especially in the mesetas, to change the distance covered by the stages, shortening them if they are too tired, or lengthening them to save time. Always remember that it is your path and to listen to your body and mind.

16th Stage_ Fromista - Carrión de los Condes
Length: 18.8 km Total height difference: 129mt

The route to the next destination is undemanding due to the flat profile. On the way, you will cross Villalcàzar de Sirga where an important church belonging to the Templar order is located, a structure of particular interest.

Once in Carriòn, you will finally be able to find the availability of services on fugitive mesetas.

17th Stage_ Carriòn de Los Condes - Terradillo de Los Templarios
Length: 26.3Km Total height difference: 234 mt

In itself it is a slightly longer stage than the others but still not very demanding, and even if the route in terms of the landscape can be monotonous, walking on the Via Aquitana at the time trampled by the ancient Romans who left from Bordeaux to reach Astorga, gives that perception of epic. However, it must be kept in mind that in this stage you will cross villages with few services, so it is good to remember to stock up on water and food when you have the opportunity. Up to Terradillo de Los Templarios, famous for the legend of the goose with the golden eggs.

18th Stage Terradillo de Los Templarios - Bercianos del Real Camino

length: 23Km Total height difference: 264 mt

this stage highlights two aspects: the first is that you enter the province of Leòn, the other with a psychologically relevant impact consists in the fact that we will pass through the city of Sahagùn, i.e. the point considered halfway between St. Jean Pied de Port and Santiago.

After Sahagùn you will find a fork, and to reach the small town of about 200 souls of Bercianos it is necessary to take the path that you will find on your left.

19th Stage_ Bercianos del Real Camino - Mansilla de las Mulas

length: 26.6Km Total height difference: 124 mt

This stage is very similar to the previous one, even in this one it is necessary to pay attention to the provisions and leave early. Until you get to Mansilla de las Mulas where you can find all the services you need, including the banks of the Esla River.

20th Stage_ Mansilla de las Mulas - Leòn
length: 18.5Km Total height difference: 303mt

We start with the aim of reaching the imposing Cathedral located in the capital of the ancient kingdom of Leòn, a city that ranks among the big cities of the journey and also among the most beautiful.

Here it might be worthwhile to stop for an extra day, useful for resting and for visiting all the attractions in the city, taking walks along the banks of the Bernesga and Torio rivers. Mingle among the many tourists and visit the great heritage that characterizes it.

The path to reach it, even if a little monotonous, is not particularly demanding, but the enthusiasm for reaching the goal will make it special anyway.

21st Stage_ Leòn - San Martìn del Camino
length: 24.5Km Total height difference: 417 mt

We leave the wonderful Leòn to face the umpteenth stage, also, in this case, the kilometers of asphalt to be faced to get out of the city will seem infinite, but compensated by the landscapes and the quiet that we will encounter later. Once in La Virgen del Camino, we will have to choose between two variants, and the historical one will be the one that will lead us to the small village of San Martin.

22nd Stage_ San Martìn del Camino - Astorga length: 23.6Km Total height difference: 444 mt

In this stage, the scenery changes and we begin to enter less built-up and more agricultural landscapes. Near Hospital de Orbigo we will find yet another variant, but in this case, both will lead us to the established destination. The city of Astorga, although not one of the big ones, is very important for the route because it acts as a crossroads between the French Way and the Via de la Plata. Furthermore, being an ancient Roman fortress, it offers interesting attractions to visit, and is also a bishopric with an interesting Cathedral of ancient origins; moreover, for pilgrims, there is the possibility of receiving any free medical treatment useful for continuing the journey.

23rd Stage_ Astorga - Foncebadon
length: 25.8Km Total height difference: 470mt

We continue our journey, entering more and more towards hilly stretches and rural landscapes, we will begin to find some important climbs but also steep descents characterized by slippery terrains where prudence in tackling them with extreme calm is essential to avoid accidents.

Until we arrive at one of the most important places on the way, it is La Cruz de Hierro. Located on Mount Irago a few kilometers from Foncebadon, it is one of the most significant points on the Camino de Santiago due to its symbolic importance. There is a strong tradition that includes a ritual that many pilgrims usually perform, which consists in carrying one, of a size proportionate to the sins one wants to get rid of, from the starting point of the Camino to the Cruz de Hierro, and a once there, it is placed in the pile of stones that supports the cross to symbolically free itself from those sins through sacrifice.

In ancient times, in place of the Cruz, a pagan temple was built in honor of Mercury, protector of the paths.

Arriving in Foncebadòn, with its 1504m above sea level, we touch the highest point of the entire French way.

24th Stage_ Foncebadon - Ponferrada
length: 26.8Km Total height difference: 1847 mt

Reaching Ponferrada won't be child's play, in fact, the important difference in height combined with the uneven terrain that characterizes this stage, which must be tackled with absolute caution, will put our legs to the test. But as usual, the commitment and sacrifice required to face the toughest stages are commensurate with the beauty of the landscapes, which in this case will be full of colors and scents from the woods.

Once in Ponferrada, you will inevitably be captured by the beauty of its majestic fortress of Roman origin. Subsequently expanded by the order of the Templars reigning over León with the aim of protecting pilgrims heading to Santiago, it makes it one of the major attractions.

Stage 25_ Ponferrada - Villafranca del Bierzo
length: 24.6Km Total height difference: 641mt

From here on, the morphology of the landscapes begins to change as well as the climate. After having previously faced stages with mainly flat and straight routes with mostly arid climates, the approach to the Galicia region that we will conquer with the following stage will involve a clear separation caused by the influence that the Atlantic currents exert on the territory.
In fact, we will find very luxuriant vegetation, in addition to a climate that changes from dry to humid, with temperatures that are less hot than what we were used to.
Villafranca del Bierzo has a certain importance for the French way, which consists in the fact that in the past the pilgrims who arrived there ill, and were no longer able to continue, also in consideration of the difficulty that characterizes the following stage, equally benefited from the indulgence by visiting the church.

26th Stage_ Villafranca del Bierzo - O Cebreiro

length: 28.7Km Total height difference: 1564mt

By now it will be clear to you that when the kilometers exceed 20 and the total height differences are so considerable, all we have to do is put our legs to the test. One of the most demanding stages together with others that we have already successfully passed before. We enter Galicia and we inexorably approach Santiago, the emotion begins to be felt more and more, however, combined with a veil of nostalgia because for better or for worse, this wonderful experience begins to reach its conclusion.

The entrance to O Cebreiro located at 1300 m above sea level, will be like in fairy tales, partly because you will probably be exhausted from the climb you have faced, and also because of how the village is made up of small circular houses of Celtic origin called " Pallozas ", some with a thatched roof, all with a breathtaking view, and if conditions permit it you can admire the sea at your feet…. Of clouds.

27th Stage _ O Cebreiro - Triacastela
length: 20.8Km Total height difference: 1520 mt

Almost a descanso (rest) stage compared to yesterday, mainly downhill and therefore to be tackled calmly. We will cross valleys invaded by chestnuts, ash trees, oaks, etc., to breathe deeply until we reach the small community of Triacastela.

28th Stage_ Triacastela - Sarria
length: 25.5Km Total height difference: 1098 mt

As soon as we leave Triacastela we will immediately find a variant, both lead to Sarria anyway, consequently you will be able to choose the one you like best, however taking into consideration that you may have difficulty filling the water bottle; therefore, fill up whenever you get the chance.

This stage will be characterized by natural and silent environments, as well as by small and suggestive villages immersed in the woods.

Sarria is usually the starting point for pilgrims who intend to do only the last 100km valid for picking up the compostela. It is therefore easy to find a large number of pilgrims here in the periods of greatest influx. A city which, apart from the remains of the fortress of the Marquises of Sarria, doesn't have much to offer except for the mass of pilgrims already mentioned.

29th Stage_ Sarria - Portomarìn
length: 22.4Km Total height difference: 1011 mt

This today is one of the simplest and most pleasant stages to go through. A bit of asphalt but then a lot of countryside and small rural villages that can be reached via small bridges from the Roman era.
From here on we will see many new faces of pilgrims taking their first steps, you will notice the difference in their new shoes, in the completely different step compared to those who already have about 700 km on their legs, in the legible expressions of those who have just started.
Furthermore, unlike yesterday's stage, it will be easy to access food during the journey that will lead us to the small and artistic Portomarìn.

30th Stage_ Portomarìn - Palas de Rey
length: 24.6Km Total height difference: 967mt

And already a month has passed since our departure, it seems like a lifetime and the memories of the previous one appears
far away, but basically it's only a month even if it seems so much more. Santiago is now around the corner and in this month many things have happened, and so many emotions have overlapped.
But let's focus on this stage which is also characterized by a bit of asphalt, but also by many pleasant white road paths to travel on. Some climb to tackle but all in all not very demanding, up to Palas de Rey where to welcome you there will be many cows famous for their high-quality milk.

31st Stage_ Palas de Rey - Arzùa
length: 28.1Km Total height difference: 1259mt.

Given the many kilometers and the significant altitude difference, it is certainly a demanding stage, but it is the penultimate stage and there is a lot of enthusiasm, columns of pilgrims heading to Santiago will accompany you on the route, and you will hear the choirs sung by the various parish and non-parish groups that travel these last kilometers. One of the most important appointments of this stage for those who love to eat octopus is certainly the fact that we will cross Melide, called the capital of the "pulpo" on the Camino de Santiago, in fact here you cannot help but taste it, at any time you pass, breakfast included.

Furthermore, having arrived in Arzùa, the pilgrims of the French route will mix together with those who come from the northern route, it will be nice to share and compare the experiences of the two routes.

32nd Stage _ Arzùa - O Pedrouzo

length: 19.2Km Total height difference: 729mt.

We feel by now that Santiago's Plaza del Obradoiro and its famous cathedral are just around the corner. At this point, we have some options, that of sleeping in O Pedrouzo which is a town with all the necessary services, and then leaving us with a similar last stop for the next day.

The other alternative, very popular with pilgrims, consists in extending the stage up to Monte do Gozo covering about 34km, and then making the last stage to enter Santiago in the early hours of the morning.

In any case, to better enjoy and savor the conquest of the destination it is good to divide it into two stages, even if Arzùa is only 38.6 km from Santiago. Yeah... at this point we won't give too much weight to the difficulty of the stages, but for kilometers and height difference, this can be defined as quite simple.

33rd Stage_ O Pedrouzo - Santiago de Compostela length: 19.3Km Total height difference: 765mt.

It is undoubtedly the most overwhelming, the one we will remember the most, the one where the weight of the backpack and the tiredness of the legs disappear to leave room only for emotions. We are about to reach the goal, some will do it at a brisk pace because they can't wait to contemplate the cathedral, while others at a slow pace, a little sorry that this adventure is coming to an end.

In any case, the entrance to the Plaza del Obradoiro will leave its indelible mark on the pilgrim and it will be almost impossible not to be moved, almost as if we had prepared that little tear right from the start.

It will be nice to let yourself go lay down and admire the Cathedral while your mind runs through all the emotions experienced during this wonderful adventure. And how many joys, but also pains, and sacrifices it took to get this far, while the thought that will prevail will surely be "I did it !!" I arrived! I believed in myself and moved my limits; therefore, I will no longer be afraid of anything because whatever there is to do... it is done!

The Magic of Santiago

Already at the gates of Santiago you will notice its greatness, understood not as a territory but for the people who arrive there.

Personally, before entering the Plaza del Obradoiro, I stop to catch my breath, necessary to deal with all the emotions that arise once you find yourself in front of the Cathedral, like when you prepare for an interview where something important is being discussed, and the meeting with the cathedral is important.

But let's see what the characteristics of Santiago are; meanwhile it must be said that among the things that remain impressive, there is certainly the fact that it is a city that wants to party, pilgrims, want to celebrate with songs and dances, you will find music and songs in all the streets, you will observe in the faces of the people you meet on the street that joy and cheerfulness not common in other places.

The city is organized to welcome the myriad of pilgrims and tourists who visit it every year, with restaurants, bars, hotels, and all the necessary services, even if during the high season it is advisable to book a place to sleep a few days in advance.

One of the most touching moments for pilgrims is represented by the mass in their honor which takes place in the Cathedral. The religious celebration of the pilgrim is very significant, above all, for pilgrims who have traveled hundreds of kilometers on foot, making many sacrifices, and who have reached the pilgrim's workshop to validate all the stamps impressed on the " Credential " to collect the famous " Compostela ".

Mass on Friday evening, the "tiraboleiros" of the cathedral of Santiago de Compostela make the pilgrim's mass unforgettable. the renowned " Botafumeiro ".

Path metamorphosis

During this journey, the metamorphosis inherent in the landscapes that characterize the French route will certainly not have escaped you.

We set off from the Pyrenees where we were welcomed by lush vegetation, fresh and full of life, at the same time we ourselves were fresh and full of energy, probably with some doubts and uncertainties, but ready to face whatever might be on our path, in a nutshell as if both the path and ourselves were there to represent birth, and life itself.

And as we traveled for kilometers, the landscapes gradually began to change in appearance, all that vegetation and its beautiful green slowly gave way to duller colors, more arid landscapes, until we reached two-thirds of the way and the mesetas, where even we ourselves begin to feel more tired, the steps are no longer light and uncertain like those of the initial stretch, we begin to feel a certain growth within us, we feel that our awareness has increased and deep down we have discovered new aspects of our being, we have become wiser and with a different mental openness than before. A bit as if this trait represents for us the final part of our own life, we have become wise and more experienced elders, but we are also towards the end of our days.

Up to the third and final part of the journey. The arid yellow landscapes give way again to the colors, and our eyes are once again filled with that luxuriant vegetation that we had encountered in the first part, even those scents that we hadn't smelled for some time are back.

We feel our steps much safer, we know when it is necessary to accelerate and decelerate, we have learned to listen to our body, and we continue to feel the weight of the backpack, but we accept it as if it were an integral part of our body.

So this is a bit as if it were the representation of a new rebirth, a new life, which differs from how far we started and has been enriched with greater experience and awareness.

We are ready to continue the journey of life with greater awareness, so that everything we are called to face, we will do it with different eyes, with a clearer mind, and consequently with better results for ourselves and for others.

Buen Camino de Vita, Pilgrim!

All stages of the French Way

distance km		place
total	missing	
	793	Saint Jean Pied de Port
5	788	Huntto
20	773	Col de Lepoeder
28	765	Roncesvalles
50	743	Zubiri
56	737	Larrasoana
65	728	Arre
72	721	Pamplona
76	717	Cizur Menor

199	594 Najera
203	590 Azofra
213	580 Ciruela
219	574 Santo Domingo Calzada
226	567 Granon
231	562 Redecilla del Camino
234	559 Castelguado
239	554 Villamayor
244	549 Belorado
249	544 Santos
253	540 Espinosa del Camino
257	536 Villafranca Montes de Oca
263	530 Alto de Predaja
270	523 San Juan de Ortega
274	519 Ages
277	516 Atapuerca
279	514 Olmos de Atapuerca
284	509 Orbaneja

415	378	San Nicolas
422	371	Sahagún de Campos
428	365	Calzada del Coto
436	357	Calzadilla Hermanillos
454	339	Reliegos
460	333	Mansilla de las Mulas
479	314	Leon
486	307	La Viergen del Camino
499	294	Villadangos
511	282	Hospital de Órbigo
514	279	Villares
517	276	Valdeiglesias
525	268	San Justo de la Vega
529	264	Astorga
533	260	Murias
538	255	Santa Catalina de Somoza
543	250	El Ganso
551	242	Rabanal del Camino

659	134 San Gil
669	124 Calbor
677	116 Sarria
681	112 Beard it
689	104 Ferreiros
699	94 Portomarin
707	86 Gonzar
713	80 Ventas de Naron
717	76 Ligonde
725	68 Palas de Rey
732	61 Casanova
740	53 Mellid
753	40 Arzua
762	31 Boavista
770	23 Saint Irene
775	18 Amenal
781	12 Glue washer
788	5 Monte Do Gozo

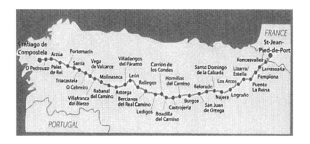

Saint Jean pied de port

Pirenei Francesi

Roscisvalle

Pirenei Francesi

Nájera

Planta del vino di Navarra

Relocado

Granón

Chapter 8

From Santiago de Compostela to Finisterre, the end of the world

Considered an extension of the Camino de Santiago, the Camino de Fisterra (or Finisterre) and Muxìa is traveled by about 15% of pilgrims arriving in Santiago by various routes.

Leaving for Finisterre via Muxìa means going to what in the past was considered the last strip of known land, and in itself this concept is exciting, but only once you get to the lighthouse of Capo Finisterre and Muxìa, both located on the costa da Morte one has that feeling of having finished one's journey, we have reached the end of the world and one cannot go further, at least on the road, it is the final epilogue of a journey that began far away, a journey that has reached the terminus.

But let's see specifically how the four stages necessary to reach the end of the world are composed.

1st Stage_ Santiago - Negreira

length: 20.4Km Total height difference: 1149mt.

Leaving Santiago we will realize that it will be different from what we entered, it is likely that we will face the next stages with a different spirit as we are aware that the main objective of arriving in Santiago has been achieved, but it will still be exciting to reach this other destination crossing the woods and rural villages that characterize this stage, which is relatively easy to tackle.

2nd stage_ Negreira - Olveiroa

length: 33.1Km Total height difference: 1215mt.

Certainly a more demanding stage than yesterday mainly due to the many kilometers to go. The completely rural environment will take us back in time, and even in this stage, there will be wooded stretches made up of chestnut, pine, and oak trees ready to welcome us and give color to our eyes.

3rd stage_ Olveiroa - Muxia

length: 31.2Km Total height difference: 1220 mt.

If it is true that this long stage will be demanding and half made up of asphalt, it is also true that today we will see the ocean for the first time, we will see the lighthouse and the sanctuary of Virxe da Barca di Muxìa, as well as its marvelous cliff where permitting, we will be able to admire the spectacular sunset overlooking the ocean. During this stage it is necessary to pay attention to the fork that we will meet after passing Hospital, the detour is for those who want to reach Finisterre without going through Muxìa

4th stage_ Muxia - Finisterre

length: 27.8Km Total height difference: 755 mt.

We are close to reaching our goal, this wonderful journey that lasted weeks or even months will end with this last stage. The goal will not only be to reach the city which in itself has so much to offer, but to go to the cape of Finisterre which is about 3km away, and set foot on the last piece of land, contemplate the sunset and observe the ocean and mixing with the sky. From there we will truly feel that we have concluded our journey, but we will also understand that we have begun another even longer one, which is that of life

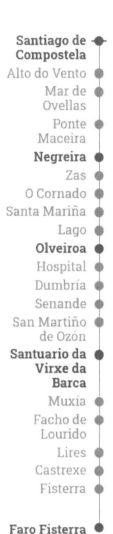

Santiago de Compostela
Alto do Vento
Mar de Ovellas
Ponte Maceira
Negreira
Zas
O Cornado
Santa Mariña
Lago
Olveiroa
Hospital
Dumbría
Senande
San Martiño de Ozón
Santuario da Virxe da Barca
Muxia
Facho de Lourido
Lires
Castrexe
Fisterra

Faro Fisterra

Conclusions

I wanted to convey all my experience gained over years of walking and trekking through the contents of this volume, with the aim of helping and giving practical advice to all those who have the desire to leave but feel held back by a thousand doubts. It sometimes happens that some obstacles are those that we ourselves create, they are limits imposed by our mind and do not always correspond to the real degree of difficulty. Taking the first step, whether in an experience such as walking, or in any other type of experience, is essential to approach what we ourselves have defined as "obstacles" to give them a more realistic vision, and better understand if this obstacle can easily be circumvented or easily overcome.

Reading this book can be considered a first step towards the journey as the topics covered are aimed at bringing real and imaginary obstacles closer, to then face them in an authoritarian and conscious way, avoiding that these are amplified by erroneous interpretations that can abandon the same project.

During my travel experiences, I have had the good fortune and the pleasure of meeting and walking alongside people who are culturally different from me, each of them with stories to tell, from the simple ones of everyday life to traumatic and significant life-changing experiences. Both have served for personal change, in fact listening to the various lives of others leads to a broader, more essential vision of the same, resulting in a lighter and more essential reading of life itself, eliminating all the superfluous that we carry around as ballast.

The experience of a journey gives so much, and the sacrifice involved in tackling it can teach us to understand that sometimes the suffering we perceive in some moments is useful for achieving happiness, that sometimes the most beautiful places and the strongest emotions are reachable through tortuous paths, but what the goal offers is clearly superior to the difficulties faced to reach it.

During my walks I understood that in addition to starting out with the right spirit, it is also essential to have the right tools. In fact, I have seen many pilgrims who, despite having set out determined to reach their goal, necessarily had to change their plans due to some technical problems encountered during the trip. Problems in most cases could have been avoided by preventing them with the right physical preparation, or with the aid of equipment suitable for the purpose. And also from there I felt the need to put in writing and transmit some fundamental precautions and useful suggestions so that those who leave for this experience do not see themselves forced to revise their plans, or as has already happened in the worst case, abandon them in progress 'Opera.

The contents of this book were made possible also thanks to the contribution of

- All the pilgrims met during the walks and their stories
- The places crossed and the people who live there
- To the web and its contents related to the journey
- All those who have passed on their experience to me over the years and provided various updates on the new technologies on the market
- To my personal trainer Antonio and his advice
- To Don Aurelio and his pearls of wisdom

Walking-Trekking-experience-2023

Made in United States
Orlando, FL
01 June 2023

33694441R00085